National parks are some of the
most magical places in the world.
Many wonderful animals call
these parks home . . .

Animals of the National Parks

AN ALPHABET BOOK BY *Fifty-Nine Parks*

Illustrations by Kim Smith
with Fifty-Nine Parks

TEN SPEED PRESS
California | New York

Aa

American bison graze together in the open fields. They are the largest mammal in the parks.

American bison are found in Yellowstone and Grand Teton National Parks.

Bb

Brown bears play in the alpine meadow. They are born the size of a small chipmunk.

Brown bears are found in Katmai National Park and Preserve.

Cc

Cougars move quietly in the colorful bushes. They are the largest cats in the national parks.

Cougars are found in Grand Canyon and Big Bend National Parks.

Dd

Desert bighorn sheep climb high for a great view. They are excellent rock climbers.

Desert bighorn sheep are found in Joshua Tree and Zion National Parks.

Ee

Elk sing with their families in the forest. Their antlers are made of fast-growing bone.

Elk are found in Rocky Mountain and Yellowstone National Parks.

Ff

Flying squirrels gracefully glide from tree to tree. They can glide the length of a football field!

Flying squirrels are found in Olympic and Mount Rainier National Parks.

Gg

Gray wolves run through rivers and streams. They can hear sounds up to five miles away!

Gray wolves are found in Grand Teton and Voyageurs National Parks.

Hh

Horned puffins enjoy the ocean air. They can dive up to 250 feet in the ocean!

Horned puffins are found in Kenai Fjords National Park.

Ii

Indigo buntings soak up the afternoon sun. They use the stars to find their way home at night.

Indigo buntings are found in Cuyahoga Valley and Everglades National Parks.

Jj

Jackrabbits sprint quickly through the sandy desert. They can run up to 40 miles per hour!

Jackrabbits are found in Death Valley and Big Bend National Parks.

Kk

Kingfishers find a cozy place for their nests. They make their homes underground and in trees.

Kingfishers are found in Grand Canyon and North Cascades National Parks.

Ll

Loggerhead sea turtles swim in the deep blue sea. They can weigh as much as a large piano.

Loggerhead sea turtles are found in Dry Tortugas National Park.

Mm

Moose stroll through the lake to find tasty plants to eat. They are great underwater divers.

Moose are found in Isle Royale and Glacier National Parks.

Nn

Northern river otters swim gracefully underwater. They can hold their breath for eight minutes!

Northern river otters are found in Great Smoky Mountains and Isle Royale National Parks.

Oo

Orcas travel together with their pods. They are the largest member of the dolphin family.

Orcas are found in Glacier Bay and Channel Islands National Parks.

Pp

Peregrine falcons perch high up in a tree. They can dive up to 240 miles per hour!

Peregrine falcons are found in Yosemite and Shenandoah National Parks.

Qq

Quail spend the day together with their chicks. Many have a plume that is called a topknot.

Quail are found in Zion and Sequoia National Parks.

Rr

Red foxes run and play in the forest. They use the Earth's magnetic field to find food.

Red foxes are found in Acadia and Yellowstone National Parks.

Ss

Snowy egrets sit peacefully in the afternoon sun. They live in marshes, ponds, and dry fields.

Snowy egrets are found in Everglades National Park.

Tt

Tufted titmice sing in the springtime! They build their happy nests inside of trees.

Tufted titmice are found in Congaree and Shenandoah National Parks.

Uu

Uinta chipmunks scurry across the rocks with ease. They are also very good swimmers!

Uinta chipmunks are found in Bryce Canyon and Zion National Parks.

Vv

Viceroy butterflies explore the beautiful flowers. They help spread pollen so plants can grow.

Viceroy butterflies are found in Acadia and Shenandoah National Parks.

Ww

White-tailed deer prance through the rocky fields. They are born with spots on their fur.

White-tailed deer are found in Mammoth Cave and Great Smoky Mountains National Parks.

Xx

Xeme fly out to sea for a tasty meal. They can take two full years to grow their adult feathers.

Xeme are found in Denali National Park and Preserve.

Yy

Yellow perch swim swiftly up the cool river. They lay their eggs in connected ribbons.

Yellow perch are found in Voyageurs National Park.

Zz

Zigzag salamanders blend in with the colorful leaves. They have a zigzag pattern on their back.

Zigzag salamanders are found in Great Smoky Mountains National Park.

The National Parks

1. ACADIA (ME)
2. AMERICAN SAMOA
3. ARCHES (UT)
4. BADLANDS (SD)
5. BIG BEND (TX)
6. BISCAYNE (FL)
7. BLACK CANYON OF THE GUNNISON (CO)
8. BRYCE CANYON (UT)
9. CANYONLANDS (UT)
10. CAPITOL REEF (UT)
11. CARLSBAD CAVERNS (NM)
12. CHANNEL ISLANDS (CA)
13. CONGAREE (SC)
14. CRATER LAKE (OR)
15. CUYAHOGA VALLEY (OH)
16. DEATH VALLEY (CA/NV)
17. DENALI (AK)
18. DRY TORTUGAS (FL)
19. EVERGLADES (FL)
20. GATES OF THE ARCTIC (AK)
21. GATEWAY ARCH (MO)
22. GLACIER (MT)
23. GLACIER BAY (AK)
24. GRAND CANYON (AZ)
25. GRAND TETON (WY)
26. GREAT BASIN (NV)
27. GREAT SAND DUNES (CO)
28. GREAT SMOKY MOUNTAINS (TN/NC)
29. GUADALUPE MOUNTAINS (TX)
30. HALEAKALĀ (HI)
31. HAWAI'I VOLCANOES (HI)
32. HOT SPRINGS (AR)
33. INDIANA DUNES (IN)
34. ISLE ROYALE (MI)
35. JOSHUA TREE (CA)
36. KATMAI (AK)
37. KENAI FJORDS (AK)
38. KINGS CANYON (CA)
39. KOBUK VALLEY (AK)
40. LAKE CLARK (AK)
41. LASSEN VOLCANIC (CA)
42. MAMMOTH CAVE (KY)
43. MESA VERDE (CO)
44. MOUNT RAINIER (WA)
45. NEW RIVER GORGE (WV)
46. NORTH CASCADES (WA)
47. OLYMPIC (WA)
48. PETRIFIED FOREST (AZ)
49. PINNACLES (CA)
50. REDWOOD (CA)
51. ROCKY MOUNTAIN (CO)
52. SAGUARO (AZ)
53. SEQUOIA (CA)
54. SHENANDOAH (VA)
55. THEODORE ROOSEVELT (ND)
56. VIRGIN ISLANDS
57. VOYAGEURS (MN)
58. WHITE SANDS (NM)
59. WIND CAVE (SD)
60. WRANGELL–ST. ELIAS (AK)
61. YELLOWSTONE (WY/MT/ID)
62. YOSEMITE (CA)
63. ZION (UT)

My National Park Memories
Use this space to record your visit with writing, drawings, and pictures.

Park I Visited (and the Date):

Animals I Saw:

Trees and Plants I Saw:

Who I Went With:

Animals I Heard:

Other Memories:

Fifty-Nine Parks
· PRINT SERIES ·

Fifty-Nine Parks is a renowned art collective known for their original poster art, which celebrates America's national parks and features the work of prominent artists from around the world. A percentage of the proceeds from their poster sales is donated to the National Park Service and the series is archived by the Library of Congress. This book was created in collaboration with Fifty-Nine Parks and *New York Times* bestselling illustrator Kim Smith.

Learn more at 59parks.net

Ten Speed Press
An imprint of the Crown Publishing Group
A division of Penguin Random House LLC
tenspeed.com

Text and illustrations copyright © 2025 by Fifty-Nine Parks, LLC
Text by JP Boneyard
Illustrations by Kim Smith with Fifty-Nine Parks

Penguin Random House values and supports copyright. Copyright fuels creativity, encourages diverse voices, promotes free speech, and creates a vibrant culture. Thank you for buying an authorized edition of this book and for complying with copyright laws by not reproducing, scanning, or distributing any part of it in any form without permission. You are supporting writers and allowing Penguin Random House to continue to publish books for every reader. Please note that no part of this book may be used or reproduced in any manner for the purpose of training artificial intelligence technologies or systems.

Ten Speed Press and the Ten Speed Press colophon are registered trademarks of Penguin Random House LLC.

Typefaces: Adobe Fonts' New Spirit and Monotype Fonts' Trade Gothic Condensed

Library of Congress Cataloging-in-Publication Data
Names: Boneyard, JP, 1982– author. | Smith, Kim, 1986– illustrator. | Fifty-Nine Parks (Firm) Title: Animals of the national parks : an alphabet book / by Fifty-Nine Parks ; text by JP Boneyard ; illustrations by Kim Smith with Fifty-Nine Parks. Description: First edition. | New York : Ten Speed Press, an imprint of Crown Publishing Group, [2025] Identifiers: LCCN 2024039468 (print) | LCCN 2024039469 (ebook) | ISBN 9780593837344 (hardcover) | ISBN 9780593837351 (ebook) Subjects: LCSH: Animals—United States—Juvenile literature. | National parks and reserves—United States—Juvenile literature. | Alphabet books. | LCGFT: Alphabet books. | Picture books. Classification: LCC QL155 .B66 2025 (print) | LCC QL155 (ebook) | DDC 590.973—dc23/eng/20241004
LC record available at https://lccn.loc.gov/2024039468
LC ebook record available at https://lccn.loc.gov/2024039469

Hardcover ISBN: 978-0-593-83734-4
Ebook ISBN: 978-0-593-83735-1

Editor: Ginee Seo | Production editor: Terry Deal
Designer: Betsy Stromberg | Production manager: Philip Leung
Copyeditor: Leni Schenkel | Proofreader: Tess Rossi | Marketer: Monica Stanton

Manufactured in China

10 9 8 7 6 5 4 3 2 1

First Edition